To Build A Home

Poetry and Prose

HINNAH MIAN

Cover and chapter illustrations by
Sarah Sklar

Poetry illustrations by Emma Dooley

Copyright © 2018 Hinnah Mian

All rights reserved.

ISBN: 172221922X

ISBN-13: 9781722219222

DEDICATION

Dedicated to all those that were given pain and told it was love.

PART I:

ON LOVING YOU

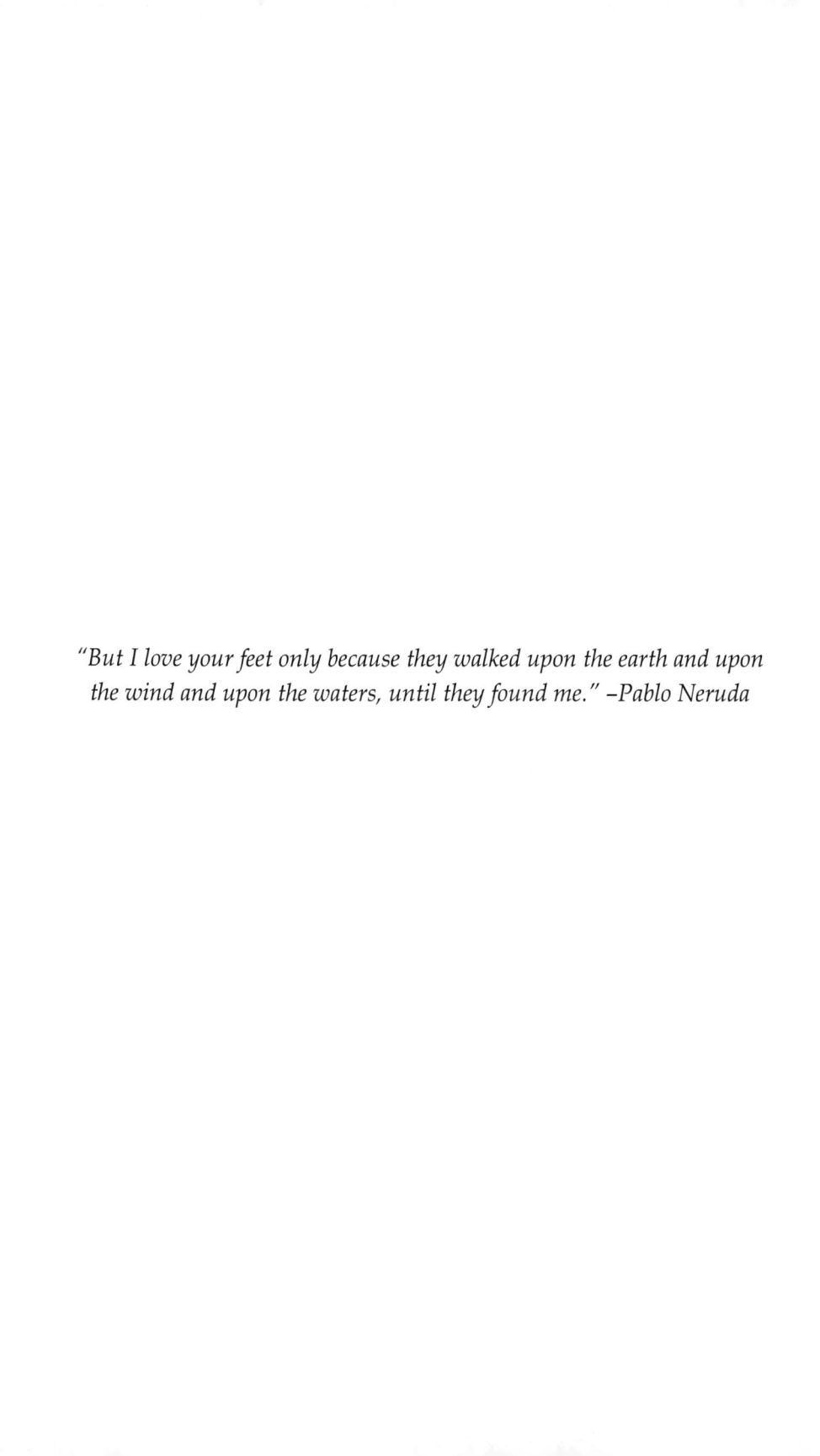

"But I love your feet only because they walked upon the earth and upon the wind and upon the waters, until they found me." –Pablo Neruda

Prologue

The first time you hit me, I didn't feel any pain.

I mean, my back was against a wall, your fingers curled around my arm, the nails digging in to my paper skin. It hurt, but at first I didn't feel the pain. I felt the fear of what this meant. Of what the watercolor bruises staining my brown skin meant. Of what the love I still felt for you meant. Of what the secrets I'd have to keep from my loved ones meant. Worst of all, I felt the unknowingness surrounding that question. The way I didn't have answers for it. The way sound struggled to crawl out of my throat as if your fingers were curled around my neck instead of my arm.

What does this mean?

What does this mean for me?

What do I do from here?

What does this mean for you?

Do you hate me?

Do you still love me?

Do I still love you?

Yes.

But how can I still love you after this?

You will never stop, you know.

So do I stay?

Either way you'll hurt.

Isn't this wrong?

Yes.

Then why don't I care?

You're in love.

But surely this can't be love?

It isn't.

Then why does it feel like it?

It is.

The pain came after. After I realized your strike stripped me of any reassurance, of any comprehension. After I realized that with the blow came the unknowingness, the fear, the emptiness. That's what hurt me.

I often described the pain as a God-shaped hole.

The marks weren't big, nor the pain heavy.

Instead, your fingers left small, purple pin prints of fear on my skin. Small enough for everyone to overlook, big enough for me to still want to hide them. But the pain the memory left was God-shaped, large enough for my body to inhale a universe of fear and burden.

Only you had the power to carve God inside of me.

Only you had the power to make it feel both divine and infernal.

But that's not where your story started, nor mine.

We started under the universe, our backs wet with the dew of the grass, our fingers pointing at the night.

Your arm touching mine felt like you were transferring some of the sky into me. I kept it ever since.

I guess this is a thank you for that sliver of sky.

And a stream of consciousness to figure out what to do with it.

Chapter 1

The Rebirth

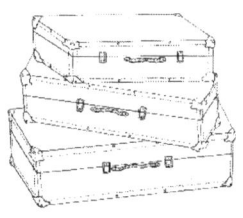

Do not love him, you told yourself. You are
still learning to grow back from the last time you were yanked
from the earth, roots and all. He had forgotten to put you in a vase
and instead carried you with him wherever he'd go. You died
because he did not nourish you, he only cherished you, and that
was not enough.

Do not love him, you told yourself. You've only just grown back
into your body. It took you four years to tape your petals back
together after you handed them to everyone you met, as if they
were business cards. You've only just gained your color back. You
do not have the capacity to love him when you are only just
learning to love yourself.

Do not love him, you told yourself. But he made love to all the parts
of you that you hated. His hands resembled those of a
gardener's — messy and calloused, but with all the intentions of
handling with care. His eyes resembled the sun and you finally
started to grow again.

I WAS WITH YOU THE FIRST TIME I REALLY LOOKED AT THE STARS AND THAT NIGHT YOU TOLD ME YOU WERE FALLING FOR MY HEART AND I WONDERED HOW YOU COULD NOT BE SO TRANSFIXED AT THE SKY AND YOU TOLD ME ITS BECAUSE YOU WANTED TO SEE MY EYES THE WHOLE TIME AND THAT NIGHT I SAW MY FIRST SHOOTING STAR WITH ITS TAIL AND WHEN YOU ASKED IF I MADE A WISH I SAID NO I FAILED BECAUSE I JUST GOT SO DAMN EXCITED THAT YOU AND THE UNIVERSE ARE REAL THAT TIME EXISTS AND IT CAN HEAL BECAUSE I NEVER THOUGHT SOMEONE LIKE YOU WOULD CRASHLAND INTO ME AND I NEVER THOUGHT BEAUTIFUL MOMENTS LIKE THIS COULD BE AND AS WE LAID UNDER THE SKY YOU ASKED IF I THOUGHT GOD WAS REAL AND I THOUGHT HE MUST BE BECAUSE THIS IS SO IDEAL

YOU KNOW ME SO WELL

one by one,

you press

my fingers

to your lips —

you know

just how

to uncurl

a fist

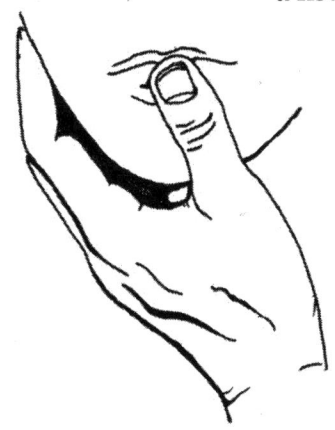

THE ROOT OF THE ROOT

I found shelter in the base of your neck,

Where I can feel your heart flutter

And I folded myself so delicately into you

That I winked out of this existence

And into another

I've built a home inside of you

Where time ticks to the beating of your heart

I've created myself a parasite

That you welcomed when

You let your lips part

I am not in my skin

I've painted myself in you

I've locked myself in your rib cage

Where my nimble hands

could never push through

TO BUILD A HOME

I exist only in terms of you

To fall out of you would be to fall apart

So I dig deeper until I carry your heart

(I carry it in my heart)

I AM A BELIEVER

I taste God every time my lips form your name — it is a worship song and every syllable in it pulsates with divinity. The heat of your breath on my neck is a hymn. When our hands are placed together I am reaching God. You are the mantra of my soul.

Kiss me again. Write scriptures on my back with your nails. Whisper a prayer in my mouth. *Oh, God.* I am a believer.

LOVELY THINGS

you are so lovely to me
my thighs turn into an array of colors
when against them your lips are pressed
i've never felt so naked
even when we're dressed

you are so lovely to me
when i undress you i see a whole galaxy
i love you in ways poets can't write
have i ever told you
you're the god damn prettiest thing in sight?

you are so lovely to me
you could be seventy-two
or just turning eighteen
but every part of you
is just so pristine

you are so lovely to me
disappearing into you
is pulling apart the stars
and allowing myself to drown
into everything that you are

SUNDAY MORNINGS

Someone once asked me what happiness felt like.

At the time, I didn't have an answer. I only said, "You just know."

Sunlight filters in like a wispy hello on a Sunday morning.

You are lying next to me, bear naked under the covers,

like a present left to be unwrapped.

Your eyes flutter open and you say nothing. You just look at me, and smile.

I do the same.

Because we both just know.

TO BUILD A HOME

"Do you want to practice?"

The song that was playing when I first told you I loved you is now playing through your speakers. You have your hand out and you're asking me to dance one late night on a school night. We're practicing our wedding dance.

If I could describe that moment I would say this:

I wanted time to be put on a perpetual loop.

I think we fabricated our own reality, my dear, because I know that we are no longer in some college dorm room. When our hands touched, our own universe spilled out.

I am suddenly in a wedding dress.

Family and friends are staring at us, but that doesn't matter. I am looking at you and thinking back to everything we've been through to get to where we are and I almost want to laugh because some days we didn't think we would make it — imagine what we would have given up.

You are in my arms and I feel like Atlas with heaven in his hands.

I'm standing on your feet because I can't dance but I don't mind because that gives me an excuse to be even closer to you.

I want the space between us to be nonexistent. I want to be so close that I melt into you.

And suddenly I am mad at whoever wrote the song because it is only four minutes and thirty-three seconds long but I want to dance with you until time erodes and we are the last two things on this planet.

　　And as long as our bodies are in this close proximity, our fabricated universe is stuck between us and reality can't spill through the cracks.

　　The song is over.

　　We let go.

~~~~~~
~~~~~

　　"Do you love me?"

　　"I do. Do you love me?"

　　"I do."

GREED

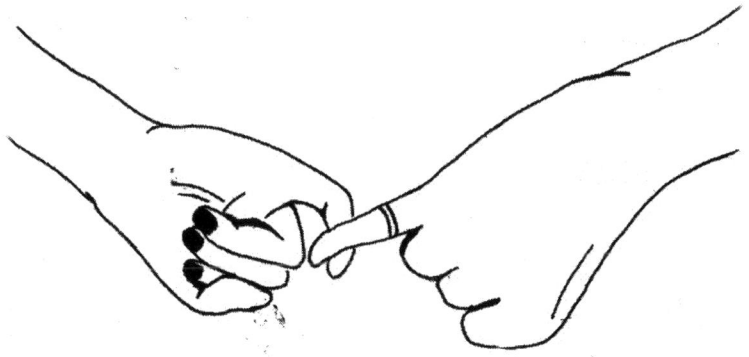

I want to be your first fulfilled promise

And the last hand you hold

I want you to be my last first

And with whom I grow old

TO BUID A HOME

I split the stars between us when I put my mouth on yours. You're two hundred and two miles away and I've built a home in the sky above your head. I will burrow myself in the thought of you until I am once more burrowed in your neck, where I am safe and vulnerable and all but brave. I like trembling when I am trembling in your arms and to build a home in your arms is to build myself anew (If you ask if I love you I do, I do, I do). I want to make ourselves into constellations so we can make ourselves into the universe where I can prove we are as infinite as we feel. And when I'm pressing my lips to yours I am writing myself in the stars. And I know I am a tangle of words and thoughts but when I think of you it's as if I've forgotten my language entirely. I know I'm not repaired but I promise I can love you endlessly — I could drain the ocean to the bottom and I'd still be carrying more love than sea. Do you know that you inhabit me like I am what you own? It terrifies me to know not a place, but a person is my home.

A PROMISE

You've repeated
    the same words
    until your voice
    has grown hoarse

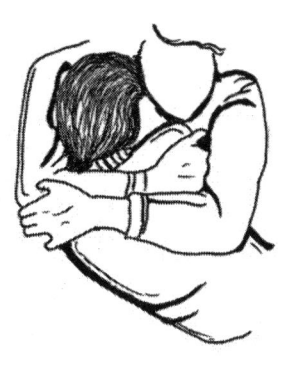

You're so scared
    that you'll lose me
    and that our love
    will run its coarse

Do not fret,
    for you cannot lose
    what will always be
        entirely yours

S'MORES

I found it surprising that you were no good at starting fires, considering you had both rage and love that could leave burns. But there we were, sitting before a fireplace, trying desperately to spark a fire so that we could make s'mores in our living room a few days before Christmas.

Smoke curled and sat in a wispy film all over the house. We coughed and sputtered and soon, I laughed and said, "It's not working."

I would've gladly made s'mores over the stove with you. In our underwear. Dancing and laughing despite the living room recovering from our failed attempt at starting a fire.

I should've known better, though.

"When have you ever known me to settle?" you said with a smile. "You want s'mores. If I have to burn down this house and roast marshmallows over the remains for you, I will."

"Why is love, something so supposedly kind, always phrased in terms of burning?"

When we first met, our knees touched.

"You kindled me, heap of ashes that I am, into fire."[1]

The conflagration that spread throughout my body and started the house fire in my skin answered the question I could never before remedy.

---

[1] Charles Dickens, A Tale of Two Cities

EARTHBOUND

Can we lie here together?

If death is still

and you are next to me

then I won't mind.

I'll lie here until

we become flowers,

until we feed the earth

and it will finally show

us gratitude.

I will lie here,

your hand in mine,

until it erodes

and becomes a part of me —

the way it has always felt.

Hours and years

are all the same —

when everything has halted

and the earth has taken claim

of our bodies, bringing us home,

greeting us by wrapping its

flowered arms around our torsos,

the two of us, laying so close

that it cannot tell your taste

from mine — then I will truly be home

    with you.

Chapter two

The Awakening

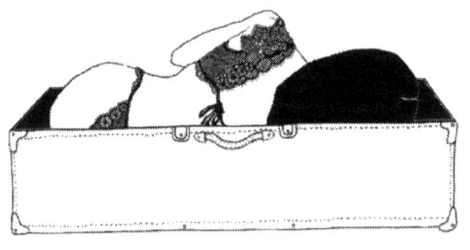

You lay on the bed sound asleep after our fight.

I am on the floor, shaking.

I wear the bruises on my arms like a warning and call it becoming.

Is this what it takes to become yours?

They color my arms like nicotine patches, but at least I'm getting my fix.

You're so peaceful when you sleep.

I curl into myself on the floor underneath you, and for all but a moment my stained arms feel like your embrace.

What is it like to love? I am in the middle of nowhere; my map has been torn to shreds. I am aimlessly wandering without a destination in mind, but I could not be further from lost. I have nowhere to go, and nowhere to be, but I am home. You are there.

What is it like to be loved in return? I am finally in my body. When you kissed me you breathed air into my lifeless soul. You painted my grey skin with vibrancy. You gently shook me awake and whispered, "You've been asleep for a long time." I woke up in a flash of brilliance.

What is it like to be scared of losing him? I am standing over a cliff. You are behind me. I cannot tell if your hand is placed on my back in reassurance or if you are about to push me.

PROMISES

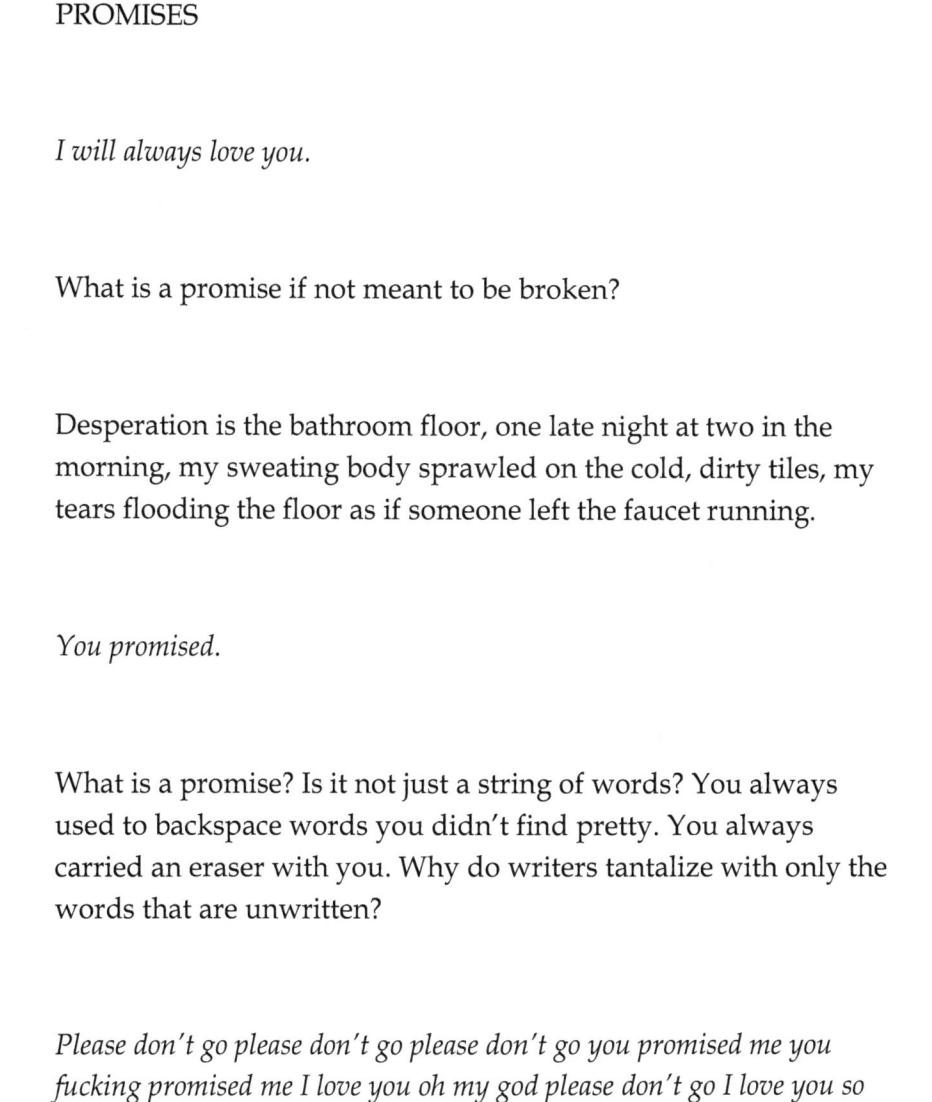

I will always love you.

What is a promise if not meant to be broken?

Desperation is the bathroom floor, one late night at two in the morning, my sweating body sprawled on the cold, dirty tiles, my tears flooding the floor as if someone left the faucet running.

You promised.

What is a promise? Is it not just a string of words? You always used to backspace words you didn't find pretty. You always carried an eraser with you. Why do writers tantalize with only the words that are unwritten?

Please don't go please don't go please don't go you promised me you fucking promised me I love you oh my god please don't go I love you so

You stayed but I think a part of me left that day

How can you mourn what you have yet to lose?

I think it is because

you take fragments of me,

mementos to keep you company,

every time you nearly leave.

My dismembered body is a trail of breadcrumbs

leading me to your promises,

and I keep trying to tell everyone:

fear not if you see me in pieces

on the street—

I am only guiding myself to him.

They don't understand.

They mourn me the way

I mourn the thought of you.

I AM UNBEARABLY HUMAN

You told me I reminded you of a superhero

but I am not made of the sun or the sea

I am more like the channels

you skip on TV

And I want so badly

to be everything you need

but I'm so sorry,

I am just made of greed

I want you to spend your whole life with me

even if I'm not everything you thought I was

but I guess love never plays out

the way you think it does

GRAVE DIGGING

My knees tend to buckle when you are near

and I pointed to you when you asked

if I had any fears

Loving me is not a scar, nor a bruise, nor a wound

I am only a body

left to be exhumed

YOU DESERVE BETTER

(An Apology)

I am in a cage,

    my wings have been clipped

    but if you had the tools to heal me

    I'd ask you to keep it

All of my feathers,

    have been dispersed

    and I'd like to apologize

    to you first

For I am just,

    a caged canary that cannot sing

    who doesn't know

    if she has weights or wings

I MISS YOU

my knees miss you making them weak

and my lips miss smiling from cheek to cheek

and i think if my arms could speak

they would say, "how do you expect me to stay vacant for so many weeks?"

my neck misses the ghost of your breathing

my heart tore out of my chest and the scars are not healing

and my fingers are trembling and are weakly asking,

"how long do i have to deal with this absent feeling?"

YOU ARE A LOVE POEM,

you are all the words

that my throat refused

to give up

You are the shaking of my hands

when they have forgotten how to hold,

forgotten how to warm up

the skin that despises to call itself

mine; the skin that treads more to you

than it ever will

to me

You are every breath

that hangs from my lips,

whispering more like an

asthmatic choke than wind,

a breath that has broken itself

like a record

and will only skip to the syllables

of your name

You are all the steps

I could not walk;

I find myself wandering to you

when I have swallowed all my maps

because I had wanted to feel the world

inside my belly

so I could finally feel

as though I belong to someplace —

I belong to you

I am yours

I am yours

I am yours

I am sorry

I could not be

a love poem, too.

PROGRADE

pro grade

adj.

Of or relating to orbital motion in the same direction as the predominant motion in an orbital system.

You were born already in pieces

and you still consider yourself an explosion

"I love you."

But the entire universe began with a bang

and planets became whole again

"You're my whole universe."

You tell me not to get within the blast radius,

that I shouldn't be part of the meteor collision

"You're my whole world."

I tell you I've always been fascinated with the sky —

I can't help but be pulled in.

TO BUILD A HOME

DON'T HURT ME

Your kisses

    electrify and

    disarm me

Your eyes

    soothe and

    alarm me

I am so terrified

    you'll heal and

    harm me

"There is a difference between absence and emptiness," she said. "For something to be absent, there has to be a lack of something that was once there before. Emptiness is just a void. You never had anything to begin with."

~~~~~~

I have a hole in me the shape of your silhouette. It aches every time you are absent from me — even if you are only gone for an hour. It doesn't realize it is only an absence. It hurts just as bad as an emptiness.

I hope every time we say goodnight, it will never turn into a goodbye.

Chapter three

The Sleep

ON DROWNING

You look for me every time you stand at the mouth of the sea.

I often let myself drown just to remind myself how lovely it was to breathe. Don't come searching for me — I know not where I am. I only know that I spell your name constantly, rearranging seashells so they will be even more beautiful when they form the curves of it. It is all that I know — like a siren's call: how alluring it sounds — and yet it wants nothing more than to grasp you by the throat and pull you down under.

This suffocation is a blanket and I yearn only to lay under it. If loving you is asphyxiation, then I will pick up a shell and carve gills into my neck.

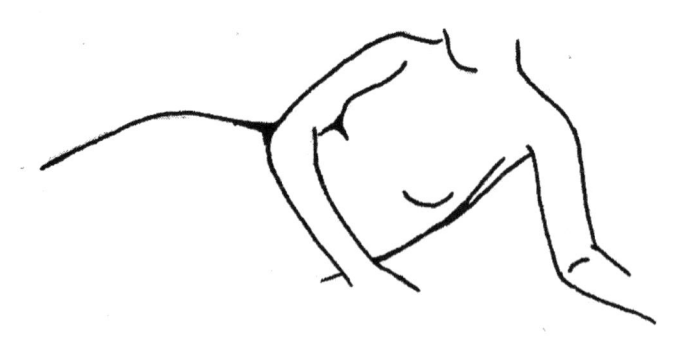

WHEN LOVE ALL BUT HEALS

I loved the night sky so much

that I allowed you to take a needle and thread

and sow your spirit to me —

thousands of little holes covered my body,

like a painter who flicked his brush on a blank canvas.

You said my body would finally resemble constellations

when the moonlight peered through me.

"Look at that," you said. *"You're so full of light."*

A GAMBLE

You've tied a noose

around my heart,

and with one end on your wrist,

you promised me forever.

I know the game of love

is but a gamble

and yet, around you,

I am all but clever.

If I wanted you

to be kind,

I would let you

cut the tether.

But instead

I wore it like a necklace,

and in a choked whisper said,

"be as cruel as ever."

HELLO GOODBYE

I was a world full of lasts

and you were my first.

How terrifying to know

that all I've ever known is goodbyes —

but yours would, by far, be the worst.

STOLKOHM SYNDROME

Keep a place for me.

I don't care where it is —

in the nook of your neck

where I'd bury my face

when being awake was

too much for me to handle.

If it's between your fingers

and hers, that's okay —

I was always just a space

to be filled.

I'll sink into

the blue bodies of bruises,

wrap myself in darkness —

call it home, call it love,

call it help.

It does not matter.

I have found comfort in

the space between

your parted lips, a purgatory —

neither heaven nor hell,

just a place to float, glad to be

somewhere near you, in you

after all:

I'll exist happily here,

make a home in

your mouth,

call your teeth bullets

and my cuts —

exit wounds.

I'll be the cigarette

burning your tongue —

exhale me, call me

comfort, call me

cancer, call me

a familiar sour taste.

If this is what

a hostage is

do not worry —

I'm not calling for help anymore.

Everything I croak out

only transforms to

the curvatures of

your name.

FROM BROKEN STRINGS TO A CONDUCTOR

You slit my throat

and tell me to sing.

I am more than just

strings out of tune,

and somehow I keep

matching pitch with you.

Tear me open

and rest inside of me.

Make a home inside

the corpse of this cello.

I'll play you a sad song

with the bow made out of my hair

and sing with a slit throat

of how I finally feel beautiful inside again.

LOVE ME BLIND

i'm not quite damaged

but i'm something adjacent

      if you're searching for something good

      then you'll just have to be patient

the truth can grab me by the throat

and i will still never face it

      i've loved you till i'm blind

      and i've learned to embrace it

GAMBIER

i.

It is only natural

for us to want to build

an everything amidst this

vast nothingness—

where cornfields replace

trees, where birds hang

from power-lines

like brown bodies.

I should have known

that we can't play god here—

we can't create

what should have

never been.

ii.

You always had a taste for blackbirds —

you spit out crows like chew tobacco,

like you love the taste of murder

in your mouth.

I am tired of you ripping off my wings

to use my feathers to floss in between your teeth.

You told me,

mouth full of skin,

"In this land,

there was nothing

to search for,

save for road kill

beautiful enough to

turn into poetry."

LOVE IN WARTIME

This

is the way

we rebuild

out of suffering.

By picking up

the bones

of rubble

and building

my city

out of tongues,

out of the currency

of songs,

after you,

my home,

took such care

to pluck my teeth out

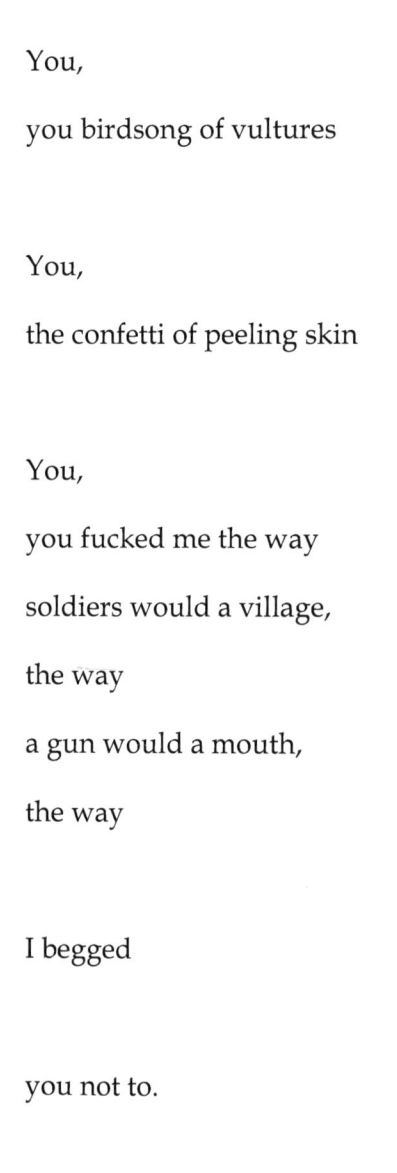

one by one.

You,

you birdsong of vultures

You,

the confetti of peeling skin

You,

you fucked me the way

soldiers would a village,

the way

a gun would a mouth,

the way

I begged

you not to.

PART II:

ON LOSING YOU

*"You can't make homes out of human beings.
Someone should have already told you that."*

- Warsan Shire, For Women Who Are Difficult To Love

Chapter One:

The Sleep

HOW TO LOSE YOURSELF

"I thought I was your home."

I have studied absence like a theory.

It is all I know how to do:

carry the bodies of those

who abandoned me

as if they are roses

I plan to give to the next

him.

I begin to resemble

every hollowed promise,

every fear that has

blossomed into a truth,

until my face contorts

into the nightmares

that embroider my thoughts.

I used to be so pretty

until I lost myself

deep within your absence.

INSIDE-OUT

"We'll be okay."

You are a breath

to be held.

A curse not yet

uttered, a secret

sitting tasteless

on a tongue.

Tell me how to love

without bones,

to love headfirst,

skin-first,

nothing but organs,

a heart beating

on the outside

so there is nothing

to hide.

I loved you in quiet

because to hide is

to pretend that

it is okay.

We are okay,

You said,

I said,

as I lay in a colorless

room, telling the doctors

that it is okay

for my heart to be

spilling from my chest.

LOVE IS BLIND

"I didn't mean to hurt you. I'm sorry I did."

I tell myself that the bruises on your knuckles

are just galaxies that I am blessed to look at.

I tell myself that it is okay that

I can see the veins

branching on your neck

when you are screaming at me

    --I hope to see flowers blossom on them one day.

I tell myself that it is okay

that you stumble into our room

intoxicated at three in the morning

because the words "I love you"

are just as beautiful

slurred.

I tell myself that it is okay

to feel so hurt,

because your kisses

are so sweet that I can no longer

taste the bitter.

On your worst days,

I still find sonnets in your half-smiles.

I LOVED EACH AND EVERY ONE OF YOUR FACES

"I was afraid to leave."

I ask, did you mean any of it?

Did you ever love me?

When you said you wanted to marry me,

did you get a bitter taste in your mouth

that you never told me about?

You say,

of course I loved you.

Of course I wanted to marry you.

You say it in a voice I can no longer recognize

and I wonder if I ever really loved

a real person

at all.

BATTLE SCARS

"I'm unlovable and I'm okay with it."

Loving you was like fighting a war —

I entered brave and left broken.

I'M ALL YOURS

"We fit like puzzle pieces."

I let myself shed my skin,

push it through a grater,

ribboning it so that

I could tie it around your wrists,

like both cuffs and a present.

Why did I let myself destroy me

so that I could be given to you?

I fell, like paper, to the floor

pooled around you,

so that you stood in

and on me.

You said you loved being

encompassed by me.

I said I loved

being yours.

ON NOT KNOWING HOW TO BELIEVE IN GOD

"I wanted to thank you for your family accepting me in a way no one has before."

Do you know what it is like to hold your name in my mouth, when my parents have always thought that I only hold God's? When they were my age, if they would have found prayers hidden between the lies and rendezvous like we had, they would have had their forgiveness burned into them. Instead, I just burned your love into my skin.

I carry the shame around me like a souvenir of our escapades, but we often prayed together, anyway. You thank me for helping you find your identity before you say goodbye to me forever. My mother curses you for taking away hers when you took away my innocence.

I have always filled the space between my thighs with divinity and I often confused your moans for prayers. I still do. I couldn't recite you a single *surat* of the Quran but if you asked me what your order was from your favorite restaurant, I'd repeat it in a heartbeat.

Dear God, I'm so sorry that we loved until we damned each other.

ON LEARNING TO LOVE A SHIPWRECK

"This bed is big enough for the both of us."

Our bodies

ebbing and flowing

on the bed,

like debris littering

the storm-riddled sea.

We crash onto and into

each other, as if

our bodies colliding

can mesh us into

something whole again.

The feel of your skin,

waves underneath mine,

is so soothing that I ignore

that we are only

floating like this

to forget that

in the morning

we drown.

I want to learn

to love

my driftwood body

without the feel of yours

on top of it.

I lay here,

back against the

sea of blankets,

reaching for the empty

space next to me,

until my bones feel

settled without

yours beside them.

ON TRANSLATING HIM

"I feel like you just never understood me."

I crave the broken love he makes to me.

The way he conveys in a lost language

of silences and curled fists

that God created this

misfit love to remind each other

how oftentimes damaged things

are to be left damaged.

I so often tried to

learn this language

just so I could talk to him

that I forgot my native

tongue entirely.

It's so hard

to choke out the

words, "I love you"

when he got the

world to curl its

fingers around

my throat.

The way he

tells me I am his —

I don't seem to mind

if it's with his lips

or his absence.

He promises me they

mean the same thing.

Learning a language

takes awhile,

I tell myself.

I don't care that

I've given

myself entirely

to his breathing —

whether it be

in her ear

or mine.

We're both just learning his language.

ALL NIGHT

"I'm never alright."

it was all darkness and teeth —

the night's fangs ripped me into

ribbons that i just tied around

your wrists

    like a present

i don't feel like a gift

when you are eating me whole,

no — i feel like the empty space

between your words

and my tongue

the empty space where all your

promises seem to drop

    like stones

i shroud myself in your absence of light

nowadays, anything feels

like a security blanket

if it is empty enough

and i have made vacancy

    like a home

your words martyr and murder me

i have peeled the ribbons of my skin

one by one and given them to

people who seem like they need more—

you always need more

    like a hunger

i am the crumbs

between your teeth

that you spit out,

falling

    like confetti

i am all night now

A EULOGY FOR THE LOVE OF MY LIFE

"I never wanted to hurt you. I really just wanted to love you."

I didn't mean to kill her.

I have often been told that I love the same way fire burns — bright, all consuming, hot and heavy…slow and painful. They don't realize they're burning until their skin peels away and they're left to look like an unrecognizable shell of their former self. Until they look in the mirror and are so afraid of what they see that they have no choice to love me more.

Don't get me wrong — I don't mean to do this. But when you've only been hurt your whole life, it's all you know how to do. Hurt back. It's like a reflex. As natural as breathing.

When she's lying on the bed, naked in front of me, I like to chart out her body like a map, placing my lips on the parts of her body I know I could destroy.

Here, her neck that I like to slit with my words.

Here, her stomach I like to fill with heavy, meaningless promises.

Here, her heart that I like to carry around just to feel the pulsating control I have over her.

Here lies the love of my life.

I'm a lover without love.

I try to extinguish it before it blazes out of control.

I'm scared of people seeing me as someone who is vulnerable enough to break.

I didn't mean to devastate you, love.

But intention and outcome are two different things.

Chapter Two:

The Awakening

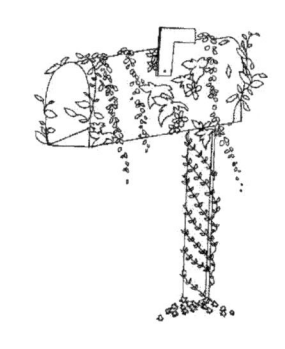

THE MORNING AFTER

"I was broken after."

I wake up feeling like I am not in my body.

I try to scrape away the feeling,

as if sandpaper can

scratch away the skin

that still

feels your touch.

I wilt the way that

forgotten flowers do,

adorned with a

letter that reads,

"I was once loved

into something

beautiful."

How do I

continue life

in a puppet

of a body

that wants nothing more

than to shed its skin?

Everyone knows

that my smile

still tastes

of your mouth,

so they do not question it

when I scrub

and scrub

until it is

gone.

HOW TO BE LOVED BY HIM

"I'm sorry for everything I put you through."

Accept that I call you beautiful, but also accept what I tell you is not.

Accept that you are not allowed to be brighter than me – exist solely in my shadow that only disappears when I turn around to look at you.

Accept that my promises are just words that I like to throw around like knives. But believe in them, anyway, the way you want to believe in me.

Accept that you are only allowed to be in my life when I feel as though I am ready to love you. Otherwise, I'll make you feel unwanted.

Accept that I was conditioned to feel broken, so that when I try to rebuild myself, I will blame you for every single thing that I will get wrong so that I still feel like I am growing.

Accept that I learned love from my mother so that I think it is the way someone runs back to you after you hurt them and hurt them.

Accept that I learned absence from my father so that I will beg and beg you to stay, but push you away so that I can ready myself for the disappearance.

Accept that I will love you so deeply and passionately, that when I abuse you, you will excuse it because you yearn for me the way an addict yearns for their fix.

Accept that I am a drug — I will destroy you from the inside out, but make it feel euphoric while doing so.

AN APOLOGY

"Tell your family I'm sorry."

"I am so disappointed in you," my mother says to me

after she learned that I let a man

touch me.

She tells me of when large men

with guns colonized her land

as she stood by and watched

her home crumble into

an aftermath.

I tell her how lies

can sound as pretty as

a promise,

how gunshots

can sound like

fireworks,

how *I didn't mean to hurt you*

can sound like,

I didn't mean to fall in love with you.

She tells me how she

was forced to live

in the comfort of her

own bomb shelter

and how it is a

disgrace that I

willingly armed

the man who

colonized my body.

I say that I am sorry

but I can no longer tell

which of us

I am saying it to.

VIRUS

"You are my home."

When I asked for you

to show the key

you showed me a

crowbar and said

that I would have let you in

anyway,

so what is the difference?

Through the key hole,

you called for God,

a deity,

a prayer,

and instead you

were met with

silence.

Where were you touched? They asked,

wanting me to point

to the parts of my body

still left bruised.

I pointed to the bedroom, called it a prayer room.

Here, where hands explored,

preying on all crevices of

a body.

The bathroom, here, where knees

met cold tile floors.

The kitchen, here, where we

started fires and danced

in the smog.

They asked if

I was okay,

if it still hurt,

and I told them

not to bother

looking for an illness

inside of me —

it is just a boy,

who made himself

at home

and never found

his way out.

LOVING YOU LIKE MY HOMELAND

"You don't understand – I don't have a place to go home to."

I talk of you the way

I remember my country —

a place I call my home

even though I am hardly

ever there.

A land I remember

in vague beautiful

images, like I am

looking at our old pictures

through misty eyes.

Your name sounds

like my native tongue —

something I understand

perfectly, but can hardly speak

because I was never taught

how to hold the words

properly in my mouth.

Your hello echoes

in my memory

like a call to prayer

cutting through the air,

a reminder not to forget

the divine love

that revived you.

I loved you

like I barely

had a land

to call my own,

a body born in between

two worlds; I can't help

that I am constantly

feeling lost —

when you left,

it was nothing new,

but left me feeling homesick

all the same.

IT ISN'T SUPPOSED TO BE THIS WAY

"I think I'll love you for the rest of my life."

i think i hate you, my love

i think i hate

every bone

that you're made up of

i'm so lonely, my dear

i hate that you left me

with nothing but

your voice in my ears

i don't want to hate you, my sweet

when you used

to be my each

morning's greet

isn't it the saddest thing?

how soulmates can

go from just that

to absolutely nothing

i think i hate you, my love

i hate that

i love every lie

you're made up of

ON FINDING YOU IN BOTTLES AND BODIES

"I started day drinking just so I could seem fine to people."

I wish I wasn't as bitter

as all the liquor

that you press to your lips.

I remember

when I was the only sin

that you liked to kiss.

Tonight I fall in love

with four strangers

who taste like you

because I've had too much to drink.

Their hands run over

the scars your love

left on me.

They don't know

that I am looking

for you in every

crevice of their bodies.

They don't know

that I want them

to touch me until

I don't feel alien

in my body again—

until I can feel

your hands

reviving what's

left of my skin.

I want to tell them,

Come,

don't be shy,

I still taste of someone else.

ON TRYING TO FEEL AGAIN

"I don't think I could ever love anyone else."

i'm sorry, i can't love you but i can miss you a lot

i can't kiss you but i can form you into a thought

i crave intimacy but i'm too scared to let it begin

i want you so much closer but i'm scared to let you in

break me, touch me, love me just a little bit

make me feel anything before i give up and quit

and when you ask me, "why are you so afraid to fall?"

i'll sigh softly, "ah, but isn't it nice to feel nothing at all?"

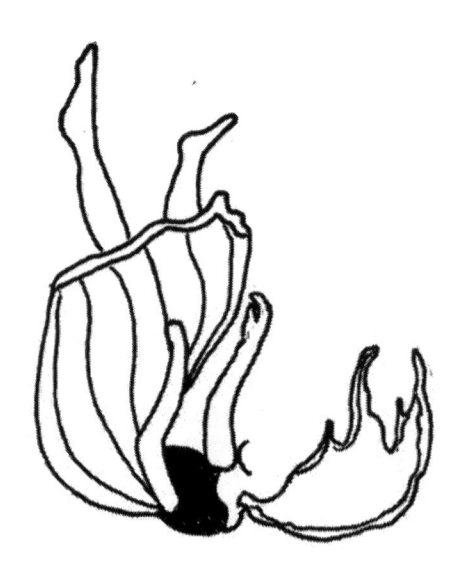

EVERYONE TASTES LIKE YOU

"Look at you. You're so beautiful. I'm so lucky."

Lately, I have been called

beautiful by dozens of

men and I have

never felt

less so.

Their words

left holes in me

the shape of your

lips

and the wind

whistled through me

to the tune

of your laugh

and I have kissed

boys who know

exactly what to do

with my body

but my body

has never felt

so hollow.

When I close

my eyes

to kiss them,

I am there again—

under the universe,

laying on your chest,

getting so excited

when a star falls

that I fail to make

a wish and I can

feel your chest

rumble with

laughter while you

whisper that you

adore me,

the stars dotting

the sky like

the golden

flecks in your eyes,

our limbs intertwining

like tree branches

embroidering the night

and in his arms,

my breath

catches in my throat

like you are saying

goodbye

all over again.

THIS DYSLEXIC LOVE

"You can trust me."

I know I often

stumble over

words when you

talk to me,

but how could

I possibly confuse

you writing *in the morning,*

I will be gone

all over my body

with your lips

parting on my bare skin,

with *I love you.*

This dyslexic love

has me rearranging

the letters of *lie to me*

to *love me*

and for a second

I confuse your pulse

for mine and it sounds

a lot like my sighs

and I am so

distracted by your

breath perfuming

my neck that I don't

hear you whispering

that I'm a fool

in my ears

and your tongue

writing *goodbye*

in my mouth

tastes like heaven

and I curse

myself for claiming

that I am a

creator of words

when I can't even read

all the red flags

that you're

scratching on my back.

THE MESSAGE I'LL NEVER LEAVE YOU

"Yeah, I'll see you around."

I heard your voice in a video today and it was only then that I realized I was starting to forget it.

It takes everything in me not to call you so I can remind myself how beautiful it is again.

I'm still dealing with your aftermath. I think I will for the rest of my life. And I want to hate you for it. Your ghost lingers in every mundane aspect of my day.

The other day I was washing dishes and I remembered how you used to yell at me while I was doing them because you'd confuse your mess for mine, the same way you often did with every mess in your life.

I'm scared to do dishes now.

But somehow I remember your smile more often than the face you made when you wanted to hurt me.

I'm not drunk yet, but I just remembered that the last thing you said to me was "Yeah, I'll see you around" and I want to cry because I know that neither of us want to see each other even though all I want to do is lie in your arms one last time.

Remember when you used to call me just to tell me a stupid joke? I heard this joke the other day and I want to leave it in your voice mail because I know it'd make you laugh but I know the thought of my voice leaves a bitter taste in your mouth that you can't wash down with liquor.

Do you do that? See something and think, *she would like this.*

Yesterday a Muslim man was beaten on his way to the mosque and I wanted to mourn with you because no one else knows how to hold me while I cry for strangers quite the way you do but I just remembered that you're a stranger now and now I'm crying for the both of you.

Hello? Are you there?

I've called to remind you how my voice sounds. I hope you still hear it in the silence sometimes, the same way I hear yours.

YOU'RE A WRITER — LEND ME SOME WORDS

"I just don't know what to say to you."

Tell me,

what is the word

for the emptiness

I feel in the middle of the night,

when I sometimes turn

around expecting

my arm to

fall across your back,

but instead just feel

the sheets that still

smell of you?

Tell me,

can language

describe what

it feels to once

be loved and now

be nothing

at all?

I look for you

in a thesaurus

but all your

synonyms just read:

sorry sorry sorry sorry

Does the English

language have a

word for how much

sorry you truly

hold in your mouth?

What is the word

for feeling your lips

in every person's kiss?

What is the word

for someone who

sucks all the words

right out of you

and replaces them

with blank spaces?

I'M SORRY THAT I FIGURED YOU OUT

"You have nothing to apologize for."

I'm sorry

you were

never properly

given love

and it made you

cold.

I'm sorry that

your heart is

a box painted

red with the word

FRAGILE

and you've spent

years building

cement walls

around it so

no one would ever

read it.

I'm sorry that

I've laid on

your chest so

often that I know

your body's language

well enough to hear

that word thumping

ever so softly

between your heartbeats.

I'm sorry that I figured you out.

I'm sorry that

you didn't know

how to handle

loving and being

loved so you

tried to rip it

and me

to shreds.

I'm sorry I let you.

THE ANATOMY OF HAUNTING

"Something just feels wrong when you're away."

I am so

    tired

of harboring

your ghost

in me.

I am so

    tired

of loving like

a wounded home

too worn and

too inhabited by

old memories

to make room

for newcomers.

You were always

the superstitious

type and I always

laughed at you when

you'd tell me that you

would never live in

a house because houses

are too easy to haunt.

I never took you seriously until now.

You made a

house out of me

and now your

touch still lingers

in between every single

one of my fingers.

Why couldn't I

see that I was

inhaling you,

giving you

permission

to possess me

when our lips touched?

Welcome home.

I didn't know

that you were

wearing me down so

you could inhabit the

cracks in my bones,

slipping in the fractures

like a mist until you

encompass me from the

inside out.

I didn't know

that you were

making a crawlspace

out of my ribcage

so I could always feel

you there —

somewhere.

Somewhere in these

walls our ghosts

are still slow dancing

in my stomach,

and with every step

I can feel it

drop further

and further

    down.

The anatomy of

this haunting

has me tearing

myself apart

limb

    from

        limb

just so I can

finally

get a chance

to see you again.

A SAD SONG

"If I learned how to sing, would you love me more?"

I find myself humming to the tune of our echo.

This is the bed where I first learned the dance of your hips, where my moans were perfectly in beat with the reverberations still haunting these walls.

Sometimes I still mistake the creaking of the old bones of this home for the way our bed mimicked our dance.

This is the record player I bought you because we always had a habit of trying to live in nostalgia.

Sometimes I still see us dancing in the reflection of that little window in the back of your room.

This is how I forget your song—

By screaming until I can no longer hear you say,

"I don't love you anymore."

Somewhere in the layers of these walls I am still smiling.

Somewhere in the layers of these walls we are waking up next to each other.

Somewhere in these walls we are still dancing.

TODAY I LEARNED THAT I AM A BOMB

"They'll always see us as different."

You were my bomb shelter.

Today I learned that people who used to smile and laugh with me in high school see me as a terrorist. Today I learned that my country doesn't want me. Today I learned that my country wants to spit me out of its teeth like tobacco, as if I am something that will rot their mouths but will provide them temporary pleasure.

I always wanted to be more than my brown skin. When you kissed me you told me I was sweet like cinnamon. I asked if I'd give you rotten teeth. You answered, "No. Just tooth aches."

There's no poetic way to describe a bomb because bombs don't want to be poetic. They want to be what fill the dead's mouths. They want to be the ashes and dust that those who didn't make it to Eid are forced to break their fast with. They want to be the prayer-mat remains of the dead.

I always wondered how I could be a bomb when you made me feel like an answered prayer.

TO BUILD A HOME

When everyone saw me as the infection that would discolor their pure white world, you made me feel like the honey that would take away a cough. When I would laugh and everyone would yell to take cover, you made me feel like I could take cover in you.

I never knew I was the bomb. But I always knew you were the bomb shelter.

Where do I take shelter now that you're gone and my own country is pointing its weapons at me?

YOU'VE MOVED ON ALREADY

"There is no one else for me. I promise."

if you love her,

don't touch her

like you touched me—

like you were always scared

our impact would break

at least one

of us.

if you love her,

don't lie to her

like you lied to me—

like you just wanted

to see me smile

for a minute

so that at night

i'd give you a

reason to

smile back.

if you love her,

don't unpack

your thoughts

in her naïve,

excited mind,

tricking her into

thinking that

love hurts.

if you love her,

don't hold her

the way you

held me at night —

as if you needed me

when in actuality

you just needed

a body.

if you love her — god,

please don't love her

the way you

loved me.

THE LAST I HEARD FROM YOU,

I had just gotten out of the hospital

and you were probably wondering

which one of your words

was the final pill

to go down my throat.

Chapter Three:

The Rebirth

OPEN LETTER TO ALL GODDESSES

Listen to me:

you have light

dripping from your pores.

You hold the sun

in your palms,

you warm souls

you have yet

to even meet.

Your tongue speaks

the language of honey,

a sweetness, a salve

people spread

on their wounds.

Young goddess,

do not give yourself

to anyone who cannot

taste, cannot see,

cannot appreciate,

the divinity in you.

You are golden.

EVEN MORE

If you get broken

into pieces

of yourself,

do not worry.

Pick up each piece

in your palm,

look at them,

and say,

"This only means,

there is even more of me

to love."

YOU ARE GOOD ENOUGH

Never again

shed your skin

to use as a doormat

for others.

Never again

pick out your bones

to build shelter

for others.

Never again

cough up the sun

living in your body

to provide light

for others.

Never again

unravel yourself

thread

by lovely

thread

to give others

your warmth.

BIRDSONG

Can you taste the prayer perching softly on your tongue?

Hold it in your mouth the way you held their names.

Let its wings expand in between your teeth

so that feathers of music drip, like gold,

between your lips.

Let your whispers form the curves of it

until song is ringing from your walls.

You must learn to love

these words the way

you held his name

in your mouth —

as if god had placed

words of honey

ever so carefully

on the tip of your tongue.

You mothered it,

let it grow until you had no

more room inside

for other languages.

TO BUILD A HOME

Look in the mirror now.

Open wide.

Do you see the prayer perching softly on your tongue?

It is your name, asking to be divinely loved, once more.

I WILL NOT CHANGE FOR YOU

You wanted me to be the black hole

to match yours

so that on my darkest days,

you'd seem a little brighter.

I am not the dark sky to your star.

I am the sun

that'll burn you

alive.

YOU ARE YOUR HOME

Lost girl,

you will not

find yourself

in other people's

eyes.

You will not

find your home

in the arms

of a stranger.

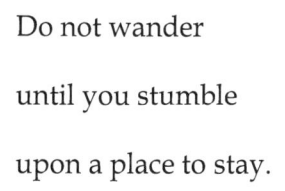

Do not wander

until you stumble

upon a place to stay.

Look in the mirror,

and say,

"You are home."

GIVE 'EM HELL

In a world where

people fear

brown skin

and women

who are comfortable

inside of it

give them something

to be terrified of.

YOU DON'T EVEN DESERVE THIS POEM

I have written

too many books

for someone who

wasn't even willing

to say goodbye to me

in more than two sentences.

To me, you were poetry.

To you, I was a page turn.

WHAT I WISH SOMEONE WOULD HAVE TOLD ME

He does not love you

if his touch

hurts you.

He does not love you

if he tells you

it was your fault.

He does not love you

if you wake up

wondering which version

of him you are going to get.

He does not love you

if after he yells at you

he begs you to stay

despite it all.

He does not love you

if he has to scare you

into not leaving.

What do you mean he hit you?

I mean, he is not who you think he is. I mean, if you act like it is none of your business, you are complicit. I mean, his white-tooth smiles are not little moons, shining bright enough so you don't pay attention to the dark. I mean, that I am made of fear and pain. That I wear hurt like a second skin. That he placed it there, molding it perfectly to my body, so that you could not tell the difference between the first and second layer. I mean, he abused me. With words and fists. Both of which hurt the same. I mean, he is a scar I will never rid of, but you look at him as if he is a perfectly designed tattoo. I mean, just because you can forget it happened, doesn't mean I can.

ENTER IT IN PEACE AND SECURITY

You once wrote a poem

about the way

sunlight entered

our room as if

it were

performing *hajj*.

You quoted

a verse

from our

holy book then,

ادْخُلُوهَا بِسَلَامٍ آمِنِينَ

enter it in peace and security.

After you left,

I crumpled

into myself,

landing on my

knees, crying, screaming

praying,

"bring him back —

if there is a God,

bring him back to me."

The earth is

now collapsing

into fall and I

have found

security in

the way the

sky is still the

sky without you

I have made peace

with the fact

that I am still

myself without you

And I am thanking God

that He brought myself

back to me.

I AM THE ASHES

I don't want to be your hero-story.

I don't want to be

the way people

say *look, brokenness*

doesn't have to be so apparent

in your anatomy — fill

the fractures in your bones

with the flesh you melted

when you flew too close

to the sun.

My pain is not

a beautiful tale

of a phoenix rising

from the ashes.

I am not the phoenix.

I am the ashes,

which can be just

as powerful.

My pain is not

a battle cry, not

a recovery song.

My blood is not

ink for you to write

your memoir with.

I am pain

and recovery

and all that is in between,

but I will not pretend

that I didn't die a hundred

times over just to get here.

Please don't romanticize my hurt

when it has become my

second skin.

LEARNING TO LOVE BOMB-THREAT BODIES

I.

Brown bodies often get confused

with mines nowadays, and

when you told me you were

scared you'd get caught in

the explosion, I didn't

blame you.

This heart resembles

a grenade and when it

bounced off the

walls in my chest

when we moved like

heat waves on the

bed, I think we both

feared for our lives.

II.

TO BUILD A HOME

I always felt dangerous

in my skin and when you

told me you found the color

of it to look more like cinnamon

than mud, you decided that

our shades of dangerous would

look even more beautiful

together.

We both taped our

gun-powdered torsos

shut with each other's

skin so that if we were

to go out in flames —

at least we'd destruct

together.

      III.

I've learned that

my body is a prayer

and not an explosion.

IV.

You treated it

like a bomb threat—

handled it tentatively,

tip-toed around me

as if you wanted

to set me off

because you

mistakenly thought

that self-destruction

is a hue of

beautiful

rather than

a hue of

tragedy.

V.

You should've

held my name

in your mouth

like a prayer.

Not a bomb threat.

You should've

treated my body

as if you were

tasting a slice

of divinity,

not treading

across a minefield.

      VI.

This brown body is

not an explosion;

it is light and honey —

all things heaven

wants to

die into.

THE REALIZATION

Loving you was so simple.

So much simpler than loving myself.

When you left, the hardest part

was realizing it was now time

for me to give to myself

what I so willingly

gave to you.

i.

Shadow: a darkness haloed by light.

A tomorrow often stalked by the knowledge

that we are just two

falling rays of sun

peeking through

the curtains of an old

hotel room.

ii.

I held you the way

light holds shadow.

iii.

TO BUILD A HOME

You, a color yet

    to be discovered.

You, a pain the

    English language does not know.

I often wonder how

blood can taste like

honey, like morning

coffee deluded with milk

like golden and warm

and all things

    you.

    iv.

I wanted to tell you

that we didn't have

to love each other like war,

like how our ancestors

would kiss

to hide in each other's

mouths when the soldiers

would march.

we don't have to be

a passed down memory.

we don't have to fight

just to exhale the

trauma from

an ancestral ghost.

v.

Let us not touch each other to prove that we are still here. Let us touch each other to forget that we are.

vi.

We are so much more

    than skin can hold.

We are cupped hands

    collecting an overflow of water from the well.

We are the screams of

    your mother, the absence of your father.

How does one love a person

    who is not a person—but a multitude?

vii.

I think we would often

rub each other's skin

to peel back layers

until we would finally

find each other

underneath all

the flesh.

    I told myself the bleeding

    was worth it.

CONFESSIONS TO MY MOTHER

I was always afraid

to tell my mother

that a man

loved me.

I was always afraid

that she'd think

my body was no

longer a home

to divinity —

that the *zamzam*

in my veins

was now tainted

with his touch.

I was always afraid

that she would know

we shared a bed,

a soul,

a home —

that her little girl

has been tasted

by a man.

I was always afraid

to tell my mother

that a man

broke me.

I was afraid

that she'd think

her little girl's

body was the site

of a losing battle.

I was afraid

that she'd think

that I gave up

my body: a temple,

a holy scripture,

to one who could not

feel the divinity

inside it.

When I told her

these things

she looked at me,

put a trembling hand

on my cheek

and said,

"*Pari,*

a man who

truly loves you

will never break you.

Not everyone

who has the

honor of speaking

a prayer believes

in the words

rolling off

their tongue."

LOVE LETTER TO MYSELF

After Ocean Vuong/After Frank O'Hara/After Roger Reeves

Darling, don't be afraid.

You have ended

so many times

only to begin again

in the morning.

Your pain is only

a burning reminder

that you have legs

that can carry you

through hell, and can

stand proudly in heaven.

Darling, are you listening?

The most beautiful parts

of your body are the parts

you had to grow again

after plucking them to put

in a bouquet for someone who

who did not have the capacity

to water them.

The man whose arms

were wide enough

to hold both you

and your shadow

were the same arms

that would tattoo

your pain in invisible

ink — so that you would

know it is there, staining

your skin, but no one else

could see it.

You would scrub and scrub

yourself raw at what looked

like your own skin —

and yet you still

asked for a second chance.

As if *chance* is something

he holds in his hands,

something you melt into,

something that will overflow

in his calloused fingers,

so that he has most of you

in his palm,

but enough to still

slip through his fingers.

Darling, you do not

need a *chance*.

Don't be afraid,

the yelling is only

the sound of people

who do not know how

to love, so they are

trying to take it from you,

someone who is made of love.

Darling, get up.

The most wondrous

part of your body

is where you will

end up, and remember

that baby steps are

still steps forward.

Here is the room

you are leaving behind—

memories of fights

and pain and what

you could have sworn

was love whistling

through you like the

tune of an old, forced

laugh. Can you see it?

You are one foot out the

door, and all you have to

do is take another

baby step.

AUTHOR'S NOTE

To Build A Home Pt II

My dear self,

I write these words not because I think they are beautiful, but because I know you are beautiful, and I want the world to know it, too.

~~~~~~

I lost a lot of things along the way.

I used to pull my bones out of my body and reconstruct them with yours, taking each and every beautiful bone of your foundation until I made myself a home out of you. Until I could feel you settled inside me. Until you were forced to unpack in my ribcage, sing yourself to sleep with the lullabies of my pumping blood, decay inside me until I would do the same.

If I could go back in time, I would tell myself:

To build a home

is not to

live and love

inside someone else

To build a home

is to look down

at your scars,

roses stemming

from your seams,

and say,

"Look, I am still alive —

in fact,

in bloom."

ABOUT THE AUTHOR

Hinnah Mian is a Pakistani-American award winning author whose work can be found on her Instagram, @hennapoetry.

Made in the USA
Middletown, DE
17 September 2023